CHRISTMAS CLASSICS

Play-Along

Recorded by Ric Probst at Tanner Monagle Studio
Trumpet: Jamie Breiwick
Alto and Tenor Sax: Eric Schoor
Piano: Mark Davis
Bass: Jeff Hamann
Drums: David Bayles

To access online content, visit:
www.halleonard.com/mylibrary

Enter Code
8470-4964-9705-2780

ISBN 978-1-4950-9701-0

Hal•Leonard®

7777 W. BLUEMOUND RD. P.O. BOX 13819 MILWAUKEE, WI 53213

For more information on the Real Book series, including community forums, please visit
www.OfficialRealBook.com

Visit Hal Leonard Online at
www.halleonard.com

Contents

BLUE CHRISTMAS

— BILLY HAYES/JAY JOHNSON

(MED.)

C VERSION

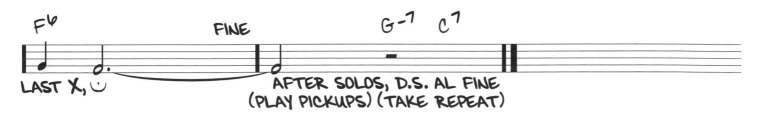

Last X, ⌣

AFTER SOLOS, D.S. AL FINE
(PLAY PICKUPS) (TAKE REPEAT)

CHRISTMAS TIME IS HERE

- LEE MENDELSON/VINCE GUARALDI

(MED. SLOW)

C VERSION

LAST X, ☺
D.C. FOR SOLOS
(TAKE REPEAT)

Frosty The Snow Man

– Steve Nelson/Jack Rollins

C Version

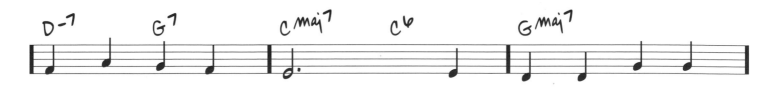

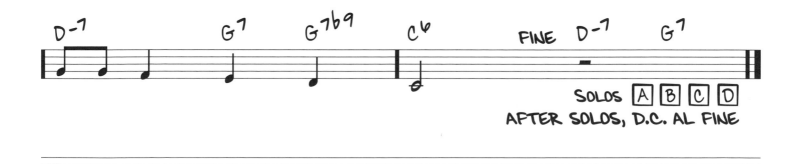

SOLOS [A] [B] [C] [D]
AFTER SOLOS, D.C. AL FINE

Have Yourself A Merry Little Christmas

— Hugh Martin/Ralph Blane

C Version

(SLOW)

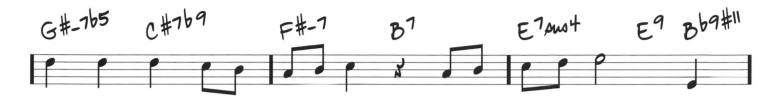

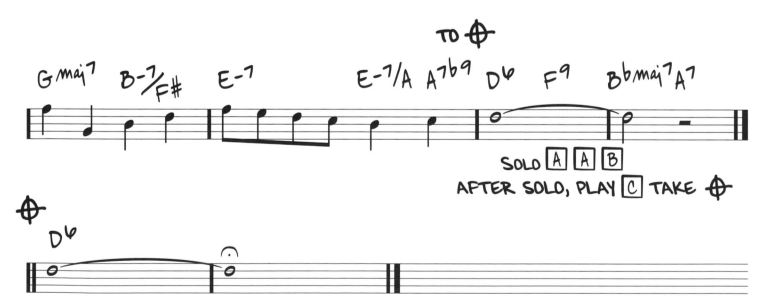

I'LL BE HOME FOR CHRISTMAS

— KIM GANNON/WALTER KENT

C VERSION

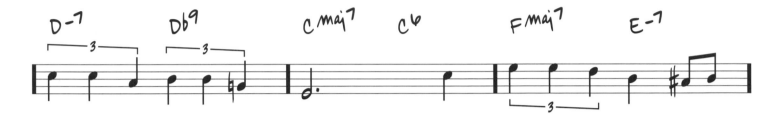

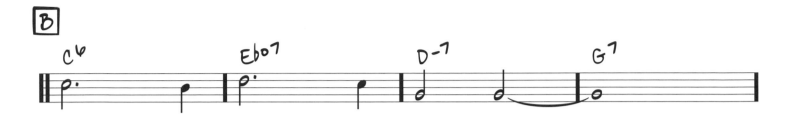

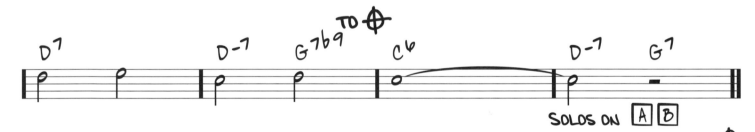

SOLOS ON A B
AFTER SOLOS, D.S. AL ⊕

My Favorite Things

– Oscar Hammerstein II/Richard Rodgers

C Version

D.C. FOR SOLOS

Silver Bells

— JAY LIVINGSTON/RAY EVANS

C VERSION

AFTER SOLOS, D.S. AL ⊕
(PLAY PICKUPS)

SANTA CLAUS IS COMIN' TO TOWN

— HAVEN GILLESPIE/J. FRED COOTS

C Version

(MED. FAST)

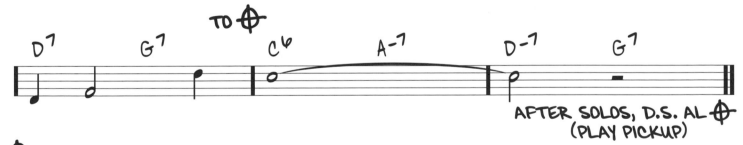

AFTER SOLOS, D.S. AL ⊕
(PLAY PICKUP)

WHITE CHRISTMAS

– IRVING BERLIN

Winter Wonderland

(MED. FAST)

C VERSION

— Dick Smith/Felix Bernard

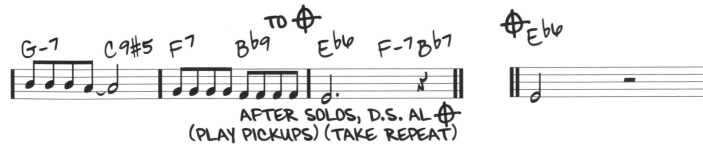

AFTER SOLOS, D.S. AL ⊕
(PLAY PICKUPS) (TAKE REPEAT)

Blue Christmas

— BILLY HAYES/JAY JOHNSON

Bb Version

(MED.)

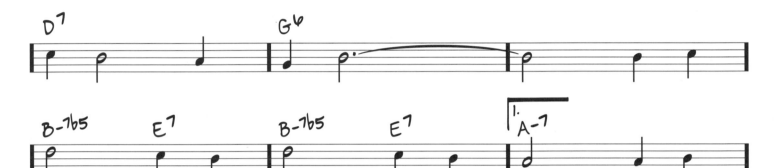
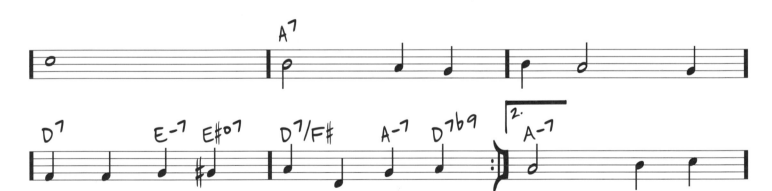

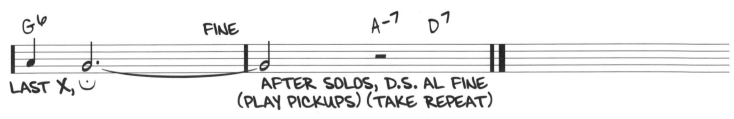

Last X,

AFTER SOLOS, D.S. AL FINE
(PLAY PICKUPS) (TAKE REPEAT)

CHRISTMAS TIME IS HERE

- LEE MENDELSON/VINCE GUARALDI

Frosty The Snow Man

— Steve Nelson/Jack Rollins

Med. Fast

Bb Version

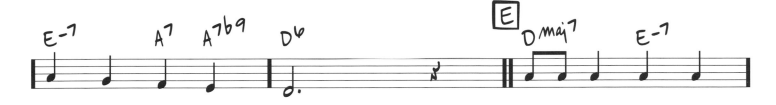

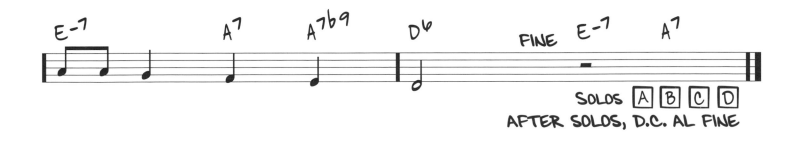

SOLOS A B C D
AFTER SOLOS, D.C. AL FINE

HAVE YOURSELF A MERRY LITTLE CHRISTMAS

- Hugh Martin/Ralph Blane

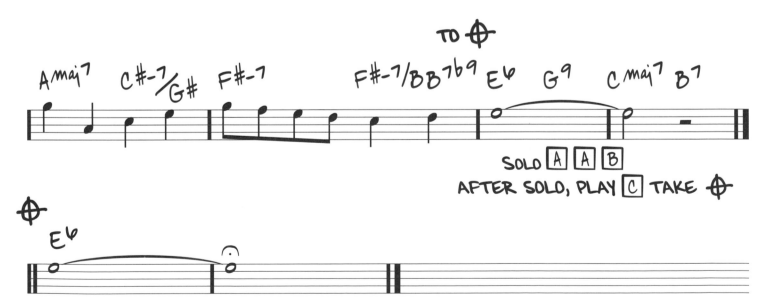

SOLO A A B
AFTER SOLO, PLAY C TAKE ⊕

I'LL BE HOME FOR CHRISTMAS

- KIM GANNON/WALTER KENT

(MED. FAST)

Bb VERSION

INTRO

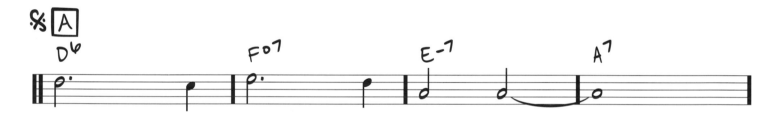

SOLOS ON A B
AFTER SOLOS, D.S. AL ⊕

My Favorite Things

— Oscar Hammerstein II / Richard Rodgers

(UP)

Bb VERSION

D.C. FOR SOLOS

Silver Bells

— JAY LIVINGSTON/RAY EVANS

Bb VERSION

AFTER SOLOS, D.S. AL (coda)
(PLAY PICKUPS)

Santa Claus Is Comin' To Town

- Haven Gillespie/J. Fred Coots

B♭ Version

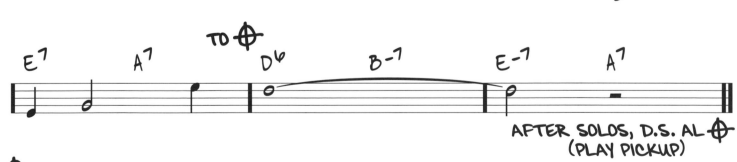

AFTER SOLOS, D.S. AL ⊕
(PLAY PICKUP)

WHITE CHRISTMAS

- Irving Berlin

AFTER SOLOS,
D.C. AL ⊕
(TAKE REPEAT)

Winter Wonderland

(MED. FAST)

Bb Version

– DICK SMITH/FELIX BERNARD

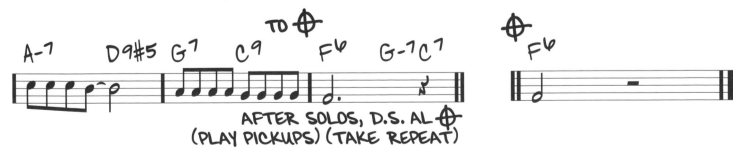

AFTER SOLOS, D.S. AL ⊕
(PLAY PICKUPS) (TAKE REPEAT)

BLUE CHRISTMAS

— BILLY HAYES/JAY JOHNSON

E♭ VERSION

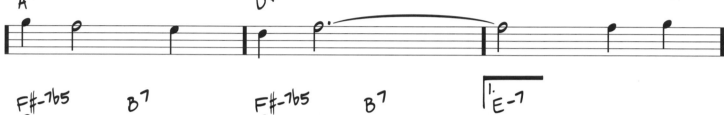

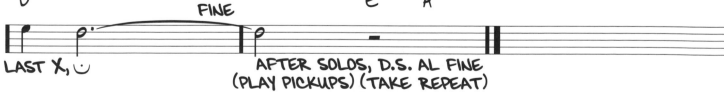

LAST X, ⌣

AFTER SOLOS, D.S. AL FINE
(PLAY PICKUPS) (TAKE REPEAT)

CHRISTMAS TIME IS HERE

(MED. SLOW)

- LEE MENDELSON/VINCE GUARALDI

Eb VERSION

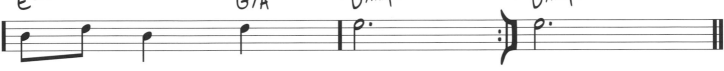

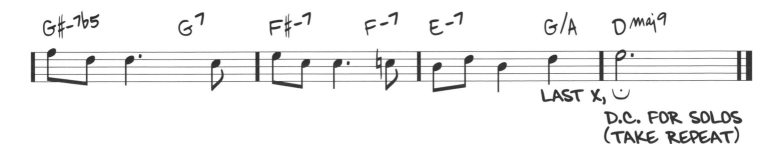

LAST X, ☺

D.C. FOR SOLOS
(TAKE REPEAT)

FROSTY THE SNOW MAN

– Steve Nelson/Jack Rollins

Eb Version

MED. FAST

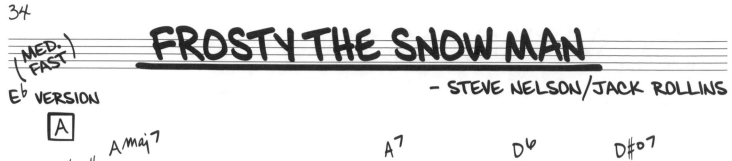

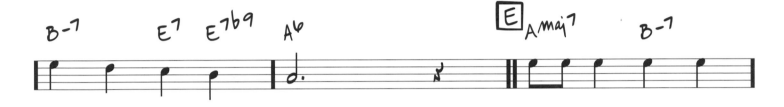

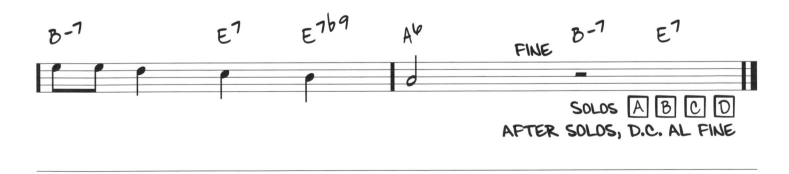

SOLOS [A] [B] [C] [D]
AFTER SOLOS, D.C. AL FINE

HAVE YOURSELF A MERRY LITTLE CHRISTMAS

- Hugh Martin/Ralph Blane

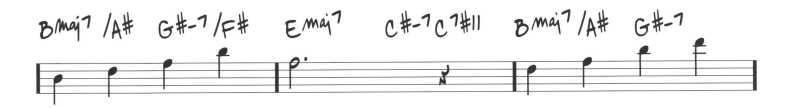

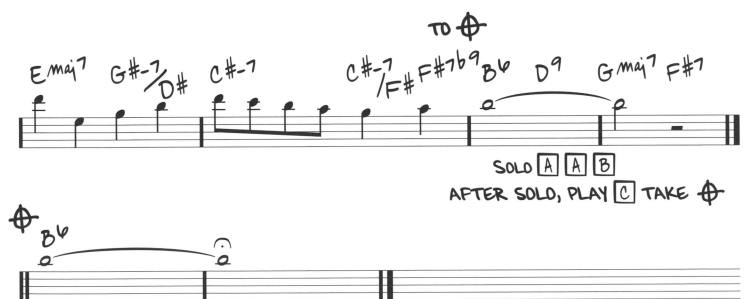

SOLO A A B
AFTER SOLO, PLAY C TAKE ⊕

I'LL BE HOME FOR CHRISTMAS

- KIM GANNON/WALTER KENT

MED. FAST

E♭ VERSION

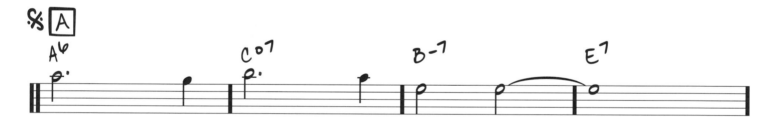

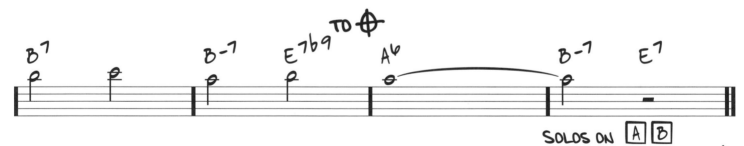

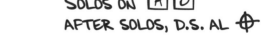

SOLOS ON A B
AFTER SOLOS, D.S. AL ⊕

My Favorite Things

– Oscar Hammerstein II/Richard Rodgers

E♭ Version

D.C. FOR SOLOS

SILVER BELLS

— JAY LIVINGSTON/RAY EVANS

Eb VERSION

(MED.)

AFTER SOLOS, D.S. AL ⊕
(PLAY PICKUPS)

SANTA CLAUS IS COMIN' TO TOWN

— HAVEN GILLESPIE/J. FRED COOTS

Eb VERSION

AFTER SOLOS, D.S. AL ⊕
(PLAY PICKUP)

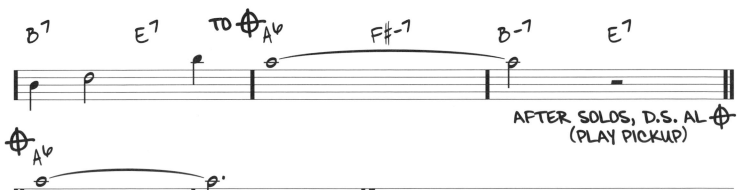

Winter Wonderland

- Dick Smith/Felix Bernard

AFTER SOLOS, D.S. AL ✛
(PLAY PICKUPS) (TAKE REPEAT)

Blue Christmas

— BILLY HAYES/JAY JOHNSON

Bass Version

(MED.)

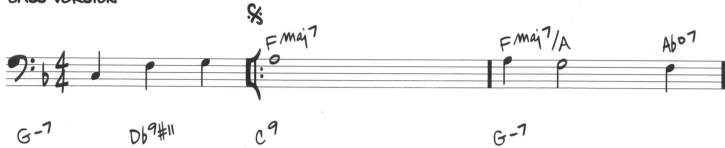

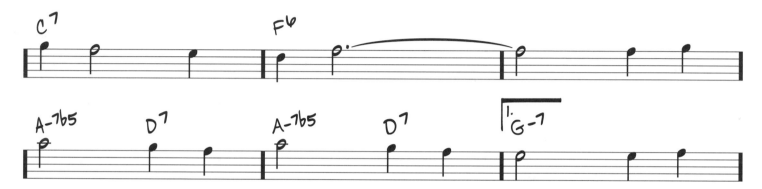

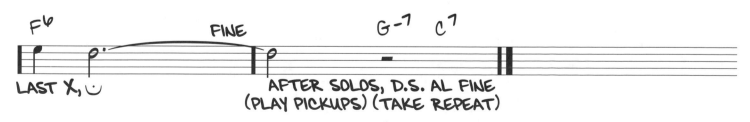

Last X, 𝄐

AFTER SOLOS, D.S. AL FINE
(PLAY PICKUPS) (TAKE REPEAT)

CHRISTMAS TIME IS HERE

(MED. SLOW)

— LEE MENDELSON/VINCE GUARALDI

BASS VERSION

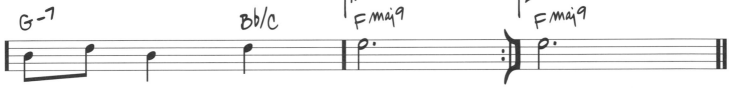

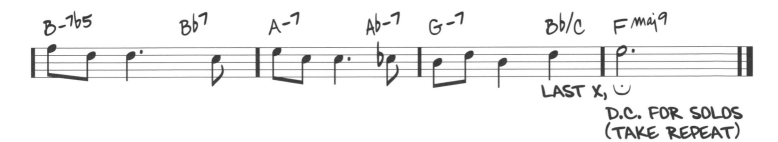

LAST X, ⌢

D.C. FOR SOLOS
(TAKE REPEAT)

Frosty The Snow Man

— Steve Nelson/Jack Rollins

MED. FAST

BASS VERSION

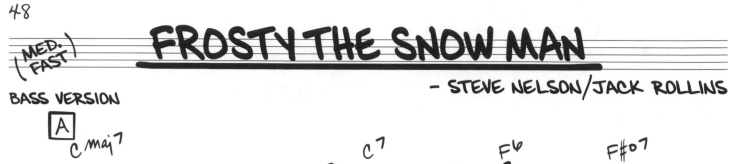

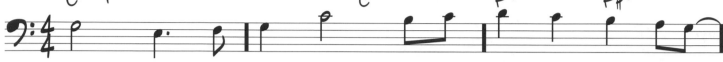

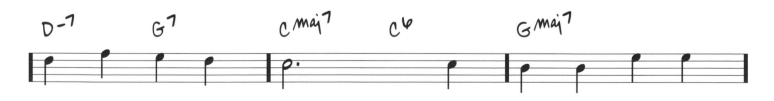

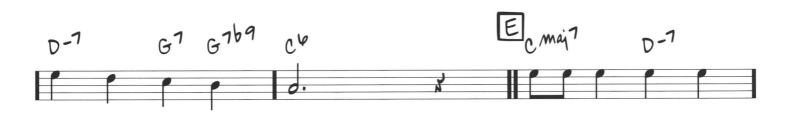

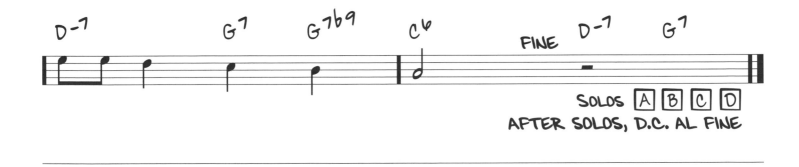

SOLOS A B C D
AFTER SOLOS, D.C. AL FINE

Have Yourself A Merry Little Christmas

– Hugh Martin/Ralph Blane

BASS VERSION

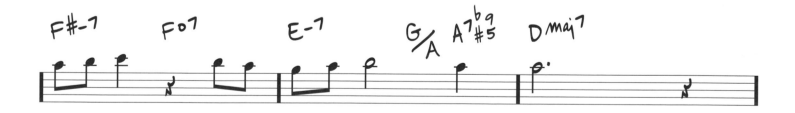

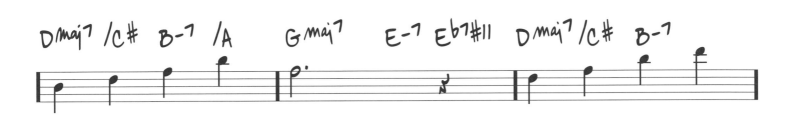

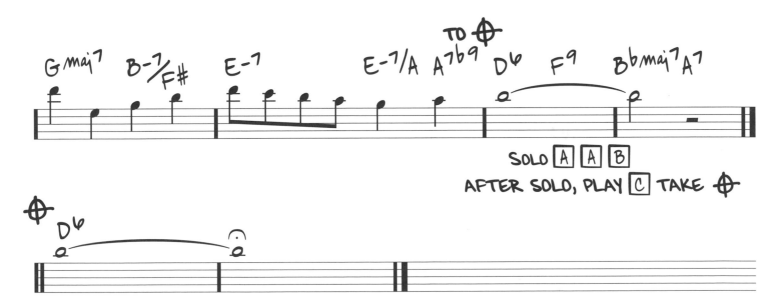

SOLO A A B
AFTER SOLO, PLAY C TAKE ⊕

I'LL BE HOME FOR CHRISTMAS

— KIM GANNON/WALTER KENT

(MED. FAST)

BASS VERSION

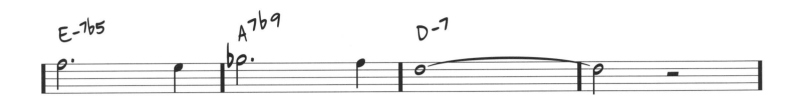

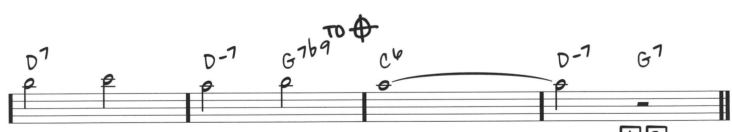

SOLOS ON A B
AFTER SOLOS, D.S. AL ⊕

My Favorite Things

– Oscar Hammerstein II/Richard Rodgers

BASS VERSION

D.C. FOR SOLOS

Silver Bells

— Jay Livingston/Ray Evans

Santa Claus Is Comin' To Town

- Haven Gillespie/J. Fred Coots

BASS VERSION

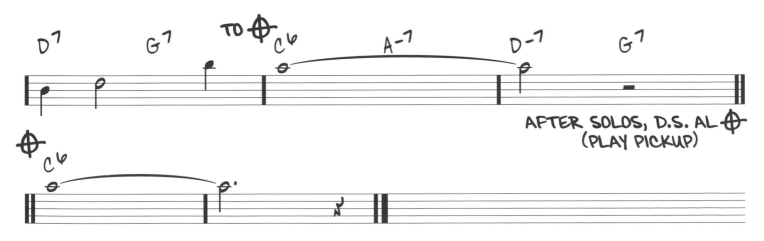

AFTER SOLOS, D.S. AL ⊕
(PLAY PICKUP)

WHITE CHRISTMAS

— IRVING BERLIN

WINTER WONDERLAND

- Dick Smith/Felix Bernard

AFTER SOLOS, D.S. AL ⊕
(PLAY PICKUPS) (TAKE REPEAT)

THE REAL BOOK MULTI-TRACKS

1. MAIDEN VOYAGE PLAY-ALONG

Autumn Leaves • Blue Bossa • Doxy • Footprints • Maiden Voyage • Now's the Time • On Green Dolphin Street • Satin Doll • Summertime • Tune Up.
00196616 Book with Online Media $17.99

2. MILES DAVIS PLAY-ALONG

Blue in Green • Boplicity (Be Bop Lives) • Four • Freddie Freeloader • Milestones • Nardis • Seven Steps to Heaven • So What • Solar • Walkin'.
00196798 Book with Online Media $17.99

3. ALL BLUES PLAY-ALONG

All Blues • Back at the Chicken Shack • Billie's Bounce (Bill's Bounce) • Birk's Works • Blues by Five • C-Jam Blues • Mr. P.C. • One for Daddy-O • Reunion Blues • Turnaround.
00196692 Book with Online Media $17.99

4. CHARLIE PARKER PLAY-ALONG

Anthropology • Blues for Alice • Confirmation • Donna Lee • K.C. Blues • Moose the Mooche • My Little Suede Shoes • Ornithology • Scrapple from the Apple • Yardbird Suite.
00196799 Book with Online Media $17.99

5. JAZZ FUNK PLAY-ALONG

Alligator Bogaloo • The Chicken • Cissy Strut • Cold Duck Time • Comin' Home Baby • Mercy, Mercy, Mercy • Put It Where You Want It • Sidewinder • Tom Cat • Watermelon Man.
00196728 Book with Online Media $17.99

9. CHRISTMAS CLASSICS

Blue Christmas • Christmas Time Is Here • Frosty the Snow Man • Have Yourself a Merry Little Christmas • I'll Be Home for Christmas • My Favorite Things • Santa Claus Is Comin' to Town • Silver Bells • White Christmas • Winter Wonderland.
00236808 Book with Online Media $17.99

10. CHRISTMAS SONGS

Away in a Manger • The First Noel • Go, Tell It on the Mountain • Hark! the Herald Angels Sing • Jingle Bells • Joy to the World • O Come, All Ye Faithful • O Holy Night • Up on the Housetop • We Wish You a Merry Christmas.
00236809 Book with Online Media $17.99

The interactive, online audio interface includes:
- tempo control
- looping
- buttons to turn each instrument on or off
- lead sheet with follow-along marker
- melody performed by a saxophone or trumpet on the "head in" and "head out."

The full stereo tracks can also be downloaded and played off-line. Separate lead sheets are included for C, B-flat, E-flat and Bass Clef instruments.

HAL•LEONARD®
www.halleonard.com

Prices, content and availability subject to change without notice.

For use with all B-flat, E-flat, Bass Clef and C instruments, the Jazz Play-Along® Series is the ultimate learning tool for all jazz musicians. With musician-friendly lead sheets, melody cues, and other split-track audio choices included, these first-of-a-kind packages help you master improvisation while playing some of the greatest tunes of all time. FOR STUDY, each tune includes a split track with: melody cue with proper style and inflection • professional rhythm tracks • choruses for soloing • removable bass part • removable piano part. FOR PERFORMANCE, each tune also has: an additional full stereo accompaniment track (no melody) • additional choruses for soloing.